THE FIRST MEN'S
GUIDE TO IRONING

Forthcoming by
E. Todd Williams

The First Men's Guide to Sewing

How to Attach a Goddam Collar Button When Your Wife Has Left You and Merger Talks Begin in Fifteen Minutes

The First Men's Guide to Housecleaning

How to Persuade Others that the Place Where You Live is Not in Need of Federal Emergency Assistance

The First Men's Guide to Childrearing

How to Get Away with Irresponsible Inattentiveness and Raise Marginally Healthy Children All the Same

THE FIRST MEN'S GUIDE TO IRONING

How You Can Survive the Decline
and Virtual Dismemberment of
Everything You Used to Depend On

E. Todd Williams

St. Martin's Press
New York

Design by E. Todd Williams

Library of Congress Cataloging-in-Publication Data

Library of Congress Cataloging-in-Publication Data
Williams, E. Todd.
    The first men's guide to ironing : how you can survive the
    decline and virtual dismemberment of everything you used to
    depend on / E. Todd Williams.
        p.   cm.
    ISBN 0-312-06973-1
    1. Laundry—Humor.   2. Men—Life skills guides—Humor.
    I. Title.
PN6231.L33W5   1992
814'.54—dc20   91-33309
                                                    CIP

First Edition

10 9 8 7 6 5 4 3 2 1

To Eluchna,
My Niam Gorf

To Monzo and Nippy,
My Etuc Gorfs

TABLE OF CONTENTS

THE FIRST MEN'S GUIDE TO IRONING

ACKNOWLEDGMENTS

Nobody helped me. Nobody *ever* helps me. I've had to go it alone my whole life long. The psychological issues here are complex and overwhelming. Is there something in me that holds others at a distance? Do they offer help that I cannot bring myself to acknowledge? Do I collaborate in my alone-ness and build a moat around my personhood?

It would be unwise for me to go much further in this line of questioning. You would begin to expect another kind of book entirely. Suffice it to say that I did all the work myself and have no other contributions to acknowledge. I hate group work of *any* kind and resent sharing credit with friends and colleagues. Like it or not, this is the way I am. Now that I'm an adult, I can say these things more freely.

INTRODUCTION

I am about to teach you how to iron.

Not because I love you or love to iron. It's because I pity you and feel an abstract responsibility to alleviate human suffering.

Face the facts. The world you thought you were going to inherit just up and disappeared. Right out the window with decent public schooling and American primacy in the consumer electronics industry. Things just happen. Nobody really *wants* declining housing values and month-by-month health insurance with ev-ery-other-Wednesday cancellation privileges by your carrier. It just can't be helped.

You probably thought it would be different. Then again, you probably thought there would always be an East Germany with Four Power guarantees of peace in our time.

All you had to do was study real hard, sign on with the right firm, and the little lady sitting next to you in B-school would stay up until midnight and iron your shirts. Just like Mommy! Amazing isn't it? She actually prefers the challenge of opening the branch office in Singapore to the nip and tuck of moving an iron around your collar buttons.

What's that you say? You'll give Mommy a call? I hate to be the bearer of more bad news, but Good Old Mom buried her trusty Sunbeam about six and a half hours after she buried Good Old Dad. You may also have noticed that she lives nineteen hundred miles away, in some sunny little retirement paradise on the West Coast of Florida. Something with a "P," like Punta-whatzit. Got out of the city right before the market collapsed, with your father's life insurance settlement and six million bucks for the two- bedroom bungalow they bought when you were five.

She's got plenty of money for dry cleaning now. So how many times can you dry-clean a mu-mu?

fig. 1. The way it used to be. Kindly wives and mothers worked hard to keep their menfolk in freshly laundered dress shirts.

fig. 2. The way it is now. With women in the working world, it is sometimes difficult for wives to be as supportive as they might prefer.

Yesiree bub, it's a new world out there. You could stand on your head from here to eternity and no one would lift a little finger to help you. The helpmate thing is deader than the Shah. It's you and that shirt of yours, alone in the universe. You can't afford to pay two bucks an item and nobody will ever voluntarily press your collar again.

Damn it to hell, you're gonna learn to iron.

CHAPTER ONE

REASONABLE EXPECTATIONS

Normal people do not iron their underwear. Psychotic people iron their underwear. It has to do with certain pathological fears, like Disorder in the Universe, or Being Ready for Anything.

I have never personally known anyone who ironed underwear, but I can report suspicious sightings in the locker room of my health club. There's a guy with a receding hairline and pneumatic tendencies who spends a lot of time before his workout brushing his teeth. There's also a lot of dabbing little hairs into place, like they're going to do a screen test when he steps onto the Stairmaster.

It's probably superfluous to state that he's 5'4" tops, with tight fittin' jeans and a red Miata. I couldn't say for certain that his fashion briefs are ironed, but he takes special care folding them into his rectangular locker bag *just so*. A guy like that spends a lot of time getting ready. "A little more starch in your G-string, sir?"

For the rest of us, this is foolishness on a very grand scale. You will never need to iron your underwear unless the Queen Mother somehow persuades you to serve her her four o'clock scones in your skivvies. It could only happen on *Pee Wee's Playhouse*. And now it couldn't even happen there.

fig. 3. No guidebook is for everyone. Some men can afford to dispense with shirt ironing entirely and concentrate their attention on other garments.

Neither should you plan to iron much else. Suits to the cleaners, pure and simple. Touch 'em with an iron at home and you'll wind up with a tacky little mess and the Power Lunch that Fizzled Disastrously. It takes a very light touch and some significant experience to wield a standard household iron on a nice wool suit. There's something in the combination that generally produces flattened fibers, a syndrome known to the trade as "Dreaded Shine." Much better to zip off to the dry-cleaning professionals; they'll take care of the screw-up *and* the reimbursement.

I feel a little more sanguine about "casual pants," or "weekenders." (Whoever invents these terms is probably the same second-grader who supplies the Pentagon with the names of military operations.) If the catalogue companies have their way, we will be wearing all-cotton wash pants for our clam-gathering expeditions for some time. Just like they do in the Kennedy compound on Teddy's birthday.

Trousers like these should never be ironed. It defeats that special old-money look that nasal little twits with platinum eyebrows break their tiny little butts to cultivate. We mean baggy knees, cuffs rolled up above fashionably decrepit loafers, and two knit pique polo shirts at least, layered for a casual game of lacrosse. Take me to your family lodge in the Adirondacks.

Some men, however, will need to iron their wash pants and it can be done, albeit awkwardly. There's just too much wrestling in the Land of Groin.

Some will *also* feel the need to iron their jeans. This is a look best suited for Saturday night line-dancing at cowboy bars in second-tier hotels. The theory is that if you take blue jeans and iron them, they turn into whatever clothes you need. You never need to wear any other kind of pants.

fig. 4. Some garments should never be ironed. If you decide to wear the skins of endangered species over your business suits, consult with a dry cleaner concerning their proper care.

There's something appealing about this monolithic standard, but it's tough as turnips to achieve at home. At the very least, it will take a very hot iron, lots of water, and a jackhammer of a forearm to achieve a classic knife-edge crease in denim. You might just as well iron your lawn mower.

Basically, you're going to be ironing shirts. Lots of shirts, over and over. Depending on your schedule and the capacity of your sweat glands, it will be anywhere from five to ten shirts a week.

God help you if you're the kind of slob who wrecks a shirt before it's barely off the hanger. Jell-O belly, armpits like geysers, and a Certain Charming Way with Soup. You'll be ironing shirts, no offense intended, until Lenin's body is shipped to Washington.

CHAPTER TWO

THE RIGHT SHIRT

Let's be honest right from the start: You should never buy an all-cotton shirt. The only people who ought to have all-cotton dress shirts are twittery Anglophiles and scions of prominent families with wicker hampers full of inherited wealth.

If your name is Cyril, buy all cotton. If you came to maturity in a bedroom like a pub—the Old Man's racquet from his school days at Choate; the green felt banner on a bamboo cane—pure cotton shirting is the only material for you.

For the rest of us, it's a freaking disaster. An all-cotton dress shirt is a mess-in-the-batter's-box. From the very first microsecond you put it on, it will take the imprint of everything you do. Lean forward to kiss your little investment banker good-bye, and you'll end up with a crease the size of the Continental Divide. Ease ever-so-gracefully into your Porsche 944, and your chest will look like those new pictures from Venus: a cross-hatch of wrinkles three kilometers deep.

Since this is a book about Ironing Everything, I should probably note in passing that cotton irons like a dream. The problem is that just as soon as you're done, it will look like you never did anything at all. You could always send it out to the local laundry, but that brings us back to the question of inherited wealth. My brother wears all cotton and looks very nice, for the five-minute interval between orange juice and the car. And he's also working off $30,000 in credit card debt, even as you read this filial tribute. They say Ivan Boesky wore all cotton during the 80s, right up until the time they put him in a nice chambray work shirt. The deal is that you can't afford all-cotton shirts, or enough of them to keep you looking fresh all the time.

What every guy needs is a nice cotton blend. If you work hard at something, it oughta show. You'll still have to iron it, you can be sure of that. And it'll take a full ironing, not some scammy little touch-up. But once you're done, it'll look like you've accomplished something. And most importantly, *you can wear it again.*

Isn't that the truth you've been waiting to hear? It's all right to wear a shirt more than once! Nobody will think that you're Homer Simpson. Nobody will think that you really belong in the Regional Service Center. As long as you're wearing something in a blend, there's at least a *chance* for a second wearing. Sounds like a pretty good deal to me, especially since you're ironing these little suckers yourself.

Beyond the basics the rest is up to you. Being the burly-intellectual-balletomane-construction-worker type, I said good-bye to broadcloth some time ago. There's something a little flimsy and sheer about the fabric. It needs an undershirt and I hate to wear an undershirt with anything. Neither can I abide the faint little glow of rosy pink or chocolate chests beneath a broadcloth shirt front.

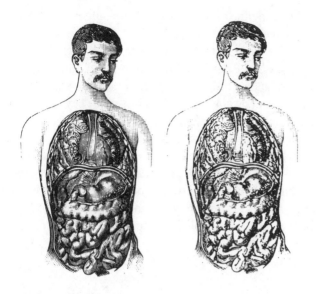

fig. 5. A broadcloth shirt is simply too flimsy to cover a man's chest without unsightly show-through. These twins have been repeatedly victimized.

My current shirt fave is a heavyweight Oxford. It's made by a well-known mail-order clothier that operates out of a small town in rural Wisconsin. It's the kind of town where nice middle-class people leave their children in the middle of the night to take orders from insomniac Yuppies in Houston. If anybody's listening over there in Dodgeville, that was as fine a piece of free advertising as you'll ever get. I'll take ten Hyde Park Oxfords, please, in 15 1/2×33. Three in blue, three in white, three in pink, and one in maize. And bring back the plum and forest-green versions.

The truth is that these shirts wear like titanium. They wash like handkerchiefs, make love to an iron, and it would take a train at thirty-five miles an hour to set a crease that you could detect a foot away. They're not for everybody (they're about six pounds each), but neither is brie studded with almonds and dark chocolate.

I have never had pilling on either collar or cuffs and I've worn some of these guys four or five times between washings. You think I *like* to iron shirts? I'm a guy just like you trying to keep going and put a couple of kids through private schools 'fore I die.

CHAPTER THREE

WHAT YOU'LL NEED

Stay calm if you can: An iron is a tool. It's in the same category of things as a power drill or a vise grip. You may *think* of it as a badge of screaming effeminacy, an all-points bulletin that you're a bleeding castrato. But you're probably the kind of man who thinks that bow hunting is for wimps. How much better and more manly to grab the deer in your hands and tear out its heart with your front incisors.

I rush to assure you that an iron is a tool, a way to get from here to there. It's not an emblem of psychic weakness or a sexual manifesto. It will not alter your genitalia as soon as you touch it. You will not wind up in a frilly little apron, sucking down bon bons and watching Oprah. An iron is an instrument, a thing of metal. Think of it as a gun you could use to kill people if you needed to.

And speaking of metal, there should be plenty of it. The world around us is shrinking and slimming. Who wants a laptop that lugs like a mainframe? Who wants a watch that's more than a sliver?

When it comes to an iron, heavier is better. Like a hammer or a saw, it should have heft and balance. You want the damn thing to take care of itself, skating along with just an occasional nudge.

fig. 6. Man kills woodland creature with ornamental growth in the middle of its forehead. Rare and endangered species *deserve* to die.

Think of that weird Canadian game like shuffle-board, played with flattened granite bowling balls on ice. One guy heaves and two other guys sweep, clearing the way for the granite clunker. That's the image to hold in your mind. You want an iron that glides like a granite clunker.

fig. 7. An iron is a tool. It should not be interpreted as a psychosexual "statement." It is just like a cement mixer or an industrial drill press. Using an iron will not make you a woman.

The problem is that you'll have a helluva time finding one. An iron used to look and feel just like it sounded. It was a piece of iron shaped for smoothing. Nowadays an iron will have a metal shoe and so much plastic in the body and handle that it'll be hard to keep it from floating to the ceiling.

I'll risk another product endorsement (and hope to

be rewarded handsomely for my generosity) and say that Sunbeam makes the best iron for the money. It's a heavy piece of business, or at least heavy enough. You want Model No. 11371. Check around wherever you live. If you can't find it there, you might as well give up. These guys used to be available through The Vermont Country Store, an old-timey outfit that merchandises New England virtue. But they disappeared out of their catalog like a bad batch of sap taps.

The real trouble is that *Sunbeam doesn't make them anymore.* I know that sounds incredible, but it's true. The best iron in our time got obsolesced. All we can hope for is a second coming, when somebody at old Sunbeam wises up to Values.

A second-tier alternative is something made by Black & Decker that used to be made by General Electric. It's another simple iron with some metal behind it that should last until something better comes along. GE made it first and then sold out. To its everlasting credit, Black & Decker left it alone.

The model you want is Z2F63D. The last time I saw one was in June of '85 at Mar-Beck Appliance in Kansas City (8223 Wornall, Kansas City, Missouri 64114, 816-523-6931). Tell 'em I sent you and remind them about my kickback.

Whatever iron you wind up buying, resist the impulse toward maximum complexity. That "Swiss Tailor's Press" in the grown-up toy catalogues looks like a first-class piece of gimcrack offal. Too big for your bedroom, too small to do the job, and too many bells and whistles for comfort. If you need a NASA manual to operate it, your iron is probably pure stupidity. Save your machismo for an Alfa Romeo.

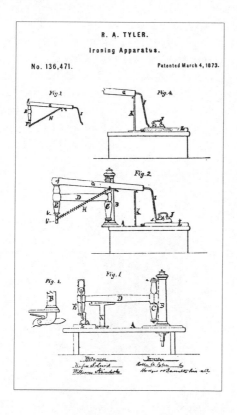

fig. 8. This iron is too complicated. Designed by R. A. Tyler, Homer Simpson's supervisor at the reactor, it is powered by Bauhaus-era neutrinos. Very rare and much the rage with collectors, but impractical.

A real-guy iron should have a temperature dial that allows it to be set for different fabrics. Beyond that it should have nothing at all. I have been tempted by models that promise an "automatic cut-off." As a catastrophic thinker, I am tortured by fear. What if I left the burners going? What if the pilot goes out in the night? What if the house fills with gas? What if I sleepwalk into the basement workroom and accidentally ignite my acetylene torch? *What if I left the iron on this morning?* So far, I have managed to resist the impulse. The models that have cut-offs are simply too light for real ironing.

fig. 9. Overwhelmed by anxiety, you may be tempted to purchase an iron with an automatic cut-off. Hold your course and resist all such counsel. The worst that can happen is that you'll burn down the house. Don't worry about memorabilia and papers of sentimental importance. Others can always be had at a price.

Skip the garbage, also, of water jets and sprayers. I have never met an iron in my life that moved water efficiently from reservoir to nozzle. You'd think it was the engineering challenge of the century to develop a capable water-carrying technology. Embedded inside each one of these failures is the leaky ruin of a New York City water main. Move the iron one way and it explodes with leaks; move the iron another way and the unit gasps. The whole thing makes me sick to my stomach and I deplore the stupidity of those responsible. Make your stand with simplicity and directness. Shower contempt on anything less.

fig. 10. A Roman aqueduct, used to move water from one location to another. The mechanism which transports water within a modern steam iron is thirty-eight times less efficient and more troublesome.

Not that you'll be able to do without water. I went through a phase where I was using spray starch to give collars and front a little touch of stiffness. Then I noticed that this made me hysterically uncomfortable; I like a shirt that is a friend to my body. Who wants to put on a cardboard box? If we were meant to wear cardboard we'd be rolls of toilet paper, shipped to our destinations in corrugated cartons.

What you need instead is a little bit of water to steam the wrinkles out of the body of your shirt. It will lubricate the iron and save you some effort. A slightly damp shirt is the shortest distance between your naked torso and Ironing Fulfillment.

My best suggestion is an inexpensive shpritzer (not to be confused with a white wine spritzer). That's the term my ethnic community uses to describe a plastic bottle that can be used to spray liquids. Some people, oddly, call it a "spray bottle." Others know it as a "pump action atomizer." People who have too much money to iron know it only from the rarefied world of indoor horticulture. In that context it is known as a "mister." If there's one in the family, it may be your "sister's mister."

In any which way, shpritzers are widely available; hardware stores have them and so do places like K-Mart. You could even tag along with some Botanical Auxiliary type and pick one up at her plant nursery of choice. Know in advance that your first one won't work. It'll have something wrong with the nozzle or the collar and you'll have to go back and buy another. Try to remember that we are late twentieth-century Americans. We get the thrusters right, but blow it on the O-rings. You might just as well buy two on the first trip.

What you want, incidentally, is something with a trigger. Do not be tempted by a press-down pump. That's the kind that forces you to squeeze downward until your index finger is bloody from the effort. If you touch one of these, you *will* lose your genitalia. Real men like a spray bottle that works like a gun. As long as it even *looks* like it could kill, it feeds something deep in the masculine psyche.

The other thing you're going to need is an ironing board. Here again, the heavier the better. What I really mean is more substantial. Ironing boards are notoriously tippy. They seem to be built for portability instead of strength. All in all, that's probably a good idea since "civilization" now means living in a featureless set of cubicles with one running foot of crown molding for every ten households. There's simply no room to leave an ironing board up. But try to avoid the flimsiest models; the last thing you want is a hot iron on your instep.

Make certain also that your board adjusts for height. The very worst thing for an iffy back is to lean slightly at the waist for more than six seconds in a row. You want a board that will easily adjust upward so that you never have to bend to guide the iron. The alternative is a board that dispenses muscle relaxants, but none has been approved by the Food and Drug Administration. Something about political pressure from orthopedic surgeons.

IRONING BOARD.
On Folding Stand.
Can be adjusted to three different heights.
$1.00.

fig. 11. The kind of ironing board you should look for. This one is a good deal at $1.00, but it is only 1 3/8 inches high. Too small for most projects. The blunt end is at the left, tapered at the right.

The last item on the list is an ironing board cover. My very first cover was a gift from my mother. It was a green and yellow floral from the people who brought us "Florida rooms." I think of it to this day as a final piece of aggression, a last-ditch effort on the part of my mother to destroy my aesthetic and transpose my sexuality.

All I've got to say is "free at last." I'm a healthy American male, age 36, with a wife and two kids and a taste for Mission Oak. I occasionally hear voices and like the look of broken glass, but people no longer refer to me as the Hillside Strangler. There are nicer ways to treat the people you love.

Back to that business of ironing board covers, get something that looks like the real you. Covers are not yet available in tartan plaids, but it shouldn't be hard to find navy blue.

CHAPTER FOUR

AN ORDERLY PROGRESSION

Every fugue needs its prefatory prelude. The same is true about ironing shirts: You shouldn't iron them without washing them first. That's probably self-evident to most people on the planet, but guides like this one assume nothing about their readers. That's what it means to be a guide: sneering condescension and thinly veiled contempt for silly persons who need to buy it in the first place.

What, pray tell, about a mint condition shirt, fresh out of the wrapper and new to the world? There are no exceptions to the general rule: All shirts should be washed before they are ironed. A new shirt has been treated to hold its shape with artificially crisp folds and rigid collar. That's why you buy it, because of its bogus promise that it will look as good on you as it does on the shelf. The trick here is something called fabric "sizing," a stiffening agent used on most new garments. Imagine the treatment as a mucilage dip. At the end you've got something that folds like paper.

The problem is that it also wears like paper. When you unwrap a shirt for the very first time, you can get the sleeves to stand out straight on their own. It's a nice special effect, but it runs counter to comfort; you don't want something that stiff on your body. Things are generally worst in the area of the collar. A man's neck is usually some version of round. It all depends on several factors—genetics, conditioning, and decrepitude among them. A turkey neck is something very much like a nightmare. There is no term in geometry adequately to describe it.

A new shirt collar, on the other hand, is a triangle. A perfect, rigid, inflexible triangle. If you think it might be fun to wear it against your neck, you might also enjoy working with a South American junta. Maybe they'll put you in the cattle prod department. Something with electrodes might also be nice.

To make a long story short, wash everything first. You can't build a skyscraper on a foundation of sand.

CHAPTER FIVE

THIS IS THE WAY WE WASH OUR CLOTHES

Welcome to the world of permanent press. The technical term in this instance is "cycle." On every washing machine manufactured within our adult lives, there is something called a "permanent press cycle." It is an approach to agitation, a strategy for scrubbing.

Nobody knows exactly how it works. Are there creatures from the sea introduced into the wash water at some especially propitious moment? Do they exude a substance which limits wrinkling and reinforces the smoothifying qualities of a blend? Is the process dependent on space/time manipulations or a domestic application of cold fusion technology?

All of these theories have been bruited about and are the subject of a new Time-Life book on the subject. The volume to consult is *Spooky Stuff That's In Your Own Basement,* the latest title in the Occult Home Maintenance series. You may not plumb the mysteries of permanent press, but bogus theorizing has its own special charms.

What's important here is that it seems to do the job. A blended fabric shirt with sufficient plasticity will do better in permanent press than anywhere else. Save the other cycles for silks and satins. You limousine liberals can wear what you like. What we're talking about here is a nice Republican blend.

fig. 12. Sea creatures suspected of a role in the permanent press cycle preferred for blended fabric shirts. Many point to the possibility of interplanetary radio waves as the operative agent.

Remember also not to pack too tight. Thirty-six shirts is packing too tight. What you want is space for the shirt to dance. You want it to catch a wave in the drum of the old Kenmore and ride it to the horizon of clean and supple softness.

If you pack too tight, you'll create a wad, the enemy of everything that a wash should be. The shirts will come out twisted and entangled, like worms in a bait bucket at the end of the day. They won't have the vitality to pull themselves apart and you'll be left to separate them into limp and exhausted individualities.

That's not so much a problem from the point of view of ironing. It is simply unprofessional and aesthetically degrading. Ten shirts at a time is the absolute max; fewer if you've got an apartment-sized washing machine. The best things in life are made in small batches, with fastidious attention to order and artistry. Balanchine never created ballets by the dozen. Neither should you wash more than a few shirts at a time.

CHAPTER SIX

THIS IS THE WAY WE DRY OUR CLOTHES

I bet I know exactly what you're thinking. "I'm thirty-seven pages in and not a word about how to iron. Is this whole process much more difficult than I thought? Or am I the victim of cynical padding, a manipulative attempt to turn a two-page article into a reasonably substantial book that will sell for $9.95 and make E. Todd Williams a very large amount of money?"

Right on both counts. Nothing is ever as simple as it seems. Take your teeth, for example; what could be easier? But one false move and it's the dentist scene in *Marathon Man*. And you thought that brushing up and down was sufficient. All *that* accomplishes is particle embediation (my term). Floss and rinse, floss and rinse. A guy who expects to iron successfully has to lay the groundwork for ironing success. Shirts don't simply materialize on the board. They have to be laid there, clean and damp, ready for the impress of hot steel on shirting.

Besides that, I need the bucks. I'm sick of this mismatch of cash and expectations. If this baby goes, I'll be on Easy Strasse. No more family trips to Osage Beach, Missouri. It's Santa Fe in September, thank you very much. A new pair of suede bucks every spring! A Waterman fountain pen in the much coveted Le Man Specialty design! I'm not asking for much, just a little slack. Enough to keep the kids in school without worrying whether we can afford sun-dried tomatoes.

Speaking of drying, it's the same stuff again. On anything but the most primitive dryers, there's a special cycle for permanent press garments. I'm assuming by now that you've gotten the message and there's no precious little cotton number in your wardrobe of dress shirts. Be a man and wear a blend.

Load a few shirts and start the machine. During the cycle, spirits from the netherworld tug gently on each fiber and smooth it just so. This is a complicated process best left to the experts. You couldn't possibly understand it if you tried. That's why we have a president and cabinet officers. Normal citizens have barely enough intelligence successfully to finish our milk and cookies. We'd never be smart enough to think up arms for hostages.

The thing to remember is to avoid overloading and also, oddly, to avoid underloading. If there's too little laundry in the Average Joe Washing Machine, the unit will promptly go centrifugal to the max. It will catch its little wad in the pocket of its cheek (so to speak) and begin lurching and bucking across the floor of the basement. Like a deb who's taken a little too much from her hip flask. Rich people produce a surprising amount of vomit.

If there's too little laundry in the Average Joe

Dryer, each garment will nuzzle against one of the interior baffles and lodge there permanently instead of tumbling. At the moment of emergence your shirts will be hot and wet, and you will feel like the ineffective sap that you are.

Not that you want everything hot and *dry*. The trick is to keep your finger on the pulse of the process. Pull your shirts from the dryer as they are rounding third base. You want most of the moisture out, without bleaching their bones. Five more minutes and they'd hit the wall: Right there is where you want to intervene.

If you go over the top, don't fret over-much. That's what your friendly shpritzer is for. It's simply easier to proceed without starting from scratch. The dryer itself will set wrinkles in your shirts. Unless you like to be brutalized, pull your shirts early.

And then hang 'em up just as fast as you can. Pull a shirt, start the dryer again, and put that same shirt on a hanger. Pull a shirt, start the dryer again, and put that *second* shirt on a hanger. If you keep the little guys tumbling, you'll get fewer deep wrinkles.

Use any old hanger for this part of the process, but don't leave a damp shirt on a wire hanger to dry. Wire is metal and metal rusts. You'll get brown marks on the shirt where most people won't see them, but they will stand as the symbol of your careless inattentiveness. Try to live your life in an affirming way. Symbols of failure will simply undercut your resolve.

CHAPTER SEVEN

READY OR NOT

Well, not *exactly*. People in the guidebook biz are fiends for nomenclature. Our stock in trade is expertise. And part of expertise is knowing what to call things. Just like at the Pentagon. A futile new weapons system which bilks American taxpayers of quadrillions is not a "hoax" or a "scam" or an "offense against nature." It's a "Peacekeeper" or a "Strategic Defense Initiative."

If you get dropped out of a plane to defend coconuts from Communists, you are not a "jerk" or a Defense Department "lackey." You are a vital component in a great democratic exercise. Knowing what to call things is an important skill. It gives us the artificial reassurance that we are "in control."

Think of me, then, as the Alexander Haig of ironing. I am "in control" and I want you to be "in control," too. The part of a shirt that lies against your back is called the **back**. (Nomenclature is so natural, you'll be doing it in no time.) In a **fitted shirt**, the **back** will be flat, a plain piece of fabric without protruding folds or tucks. In a **full-cut shirt** (normal people wear these), you'll see a **back box pleat** in the center toward the top. The purpose of a **box pleat** is extra fabric; you've got more than you really need to cover your back. The advantage is that the shirt billows slightly to the rear. If you're the kind of guy whose belly billows slightly *forward,* you're a numero uno candidate for a **full-cut shirt.**

Just above the **box pleat** (or the back panel in a fitted shirt) is a separate piece of fabric called the **yoke.** In every instance the **yoke** will be doubled: two layers of fabric instead of one. I'm guessing that this provides some structural stability, but I couldn't really tell you if my life depended on it. If I knew all the answers, I'd really be an expert and I'd be *making* shirts instead of ironing them.

The **yoke** sits right below your neck and covers your shoulders to the tops of your arms. I just took six different shirts from my closet and noticed that the best one has a kind of **split** or **duplex yoke**: two pieces of doubled fabric sewn together in the middle. This is either a fit-and-structural-stability thing or a cost-saving measure on the part of the manufacturer. ("If I use *this* little scrap and *this* little scrap, I won't have to invest in one *big* scrap.")

The little loop sewn to the bottom of the **yoke** has a number of charming and colorful names. When I was a boy, we called it a **fruit loop** and the idea was to snatch it off the shirt of a friend. This drove all of our mothers insane, because a successful snatch destroyed the shirt. All of the mothers then banded together and prevented us from having fun ever again. This is why we hate our mothers and never call them except on major national holidays. Little things sometimes have important consequences.

The **fruit loop** (or "**locker loop**") has absolutely

no function at all, at least none that I can see. It's a leftover something, a vestigial gland from some ancient phylum of male torso coverings. We were *right* to try to remove it from our shirts. It was sartorial appendectomy in the surgical wing of the fourth grade psyche of American boyhood; our mothers never understood the rightness of it all.

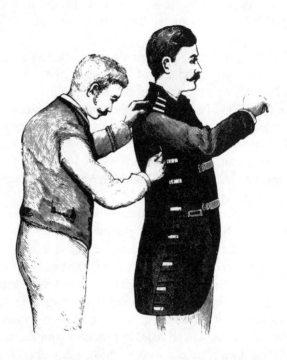

fig. 13. A tailor fondles the yoke of his client's jacket as he purports to mark a seam for adjustment.

There was a rumor once that Diana Vreeland, the former editor of *Vogue* magazine and legendary special consultant to the Costume Institute of the Metropolitan Museum, knew the original function of the **fruit loop.** If that is so, we are utterly lost. Vreeland died in 1989, the victim of a freak accident involving a life-sized mannequin, sculpted to resemble the late Prince of Wales.

The front of the shirt is called the **front**. (I told you you'd catch on to the terminology thing.) The **front** is really the part that means business. It's the part that people see and is a sure sign of breeding. Well-ironed and unwrinkled, it will evoke murmurs of approval: "What a nice man you are! How charming and sophisticated! Let's get together and re-capitalize your business. Where did I put all those interest-free loans?" If the **front** looks like hell, you will be heaped with abuse: "That was a brilliant presentation, but you look like a public toilet. Call me again after the wars of Gog and Magog. And what's that fungal growth on your gums?"

As important as it is, the **front** is also complex: two moving parts, doo-dads and whatz-its, and the general look of too many things happening at once. As you face the shirt it will be open down the middle, each side terminating at the bottom in **tails**. These are the **front tails** (your first oxymoron today!), as opposed to the **back tails.**

On the left side of the **front** is a line of seven **buttons**. If the shirt's too expensive, there might be an extra, tacked for security to the bottom of the front panel. If the **buttons** are on the right, you're in very big trouble.

It means that you're a woman and *you've been wearing blouses*. Call the Masculinity Brigade at once. They will be glad to transfer the **buttons** immediately and enter into a promising therapeutic relationship. One way or another, they'll help you out.

fig. 14. Swedish man wearing shirt, front and back views. "The yoke's on you."

On the right is a smooth little strip called the **placket.** It should have the same number of holes as the opposite side has **buttons**. Like the **yoke** discussed above, the **placket** is a doubled corridor of fabric. Here

I feel certain that we're dealing with structure. A well-constructed **placket** heavy enough for the purpose seems to draw things together and hold the shirt in shape.

You will be tempted to spend lots of time ironing in this area, on the mistaken impression that the **placket** really counts. Remember, however, that your tie will cover it. That seems a shame, but it can't be helped. The only real reason for **Placket Frenzy** is a preference for bow ties over other forms of neckwear. If that's your pleasure, iron with vigor. The same is true if you're ironing a dress-tailored sports shirt. The look of the **placket** will define the look of the shirt.

The other feature of the standard shirt **front** is a **breast pocket** to the right of the **placket** panel. There should be one **pocket** only on a standard dress shirt. And it should be open at the top, without a **button** or a flap. What you want to see is a plain patch of fabric, with no special little **button holes** or compartments for pens. A better **pocket** will be triangulated at the top with a doubled area known as **backstitching**. A shirt with two **pockets** is not a dress shirt. A shirt with **epaulets** is not a dress shirt. A shirt with stitching in a contrasting color may be just the thing in Bucharest or downtown Albania, but it is not a standard American dress shirt. Follow the rules and you will be rewarded.

The **sleeves** of a shirt are significantly less complicated. There ought to be two of them and they ought to be full-length. And they ought to attach at an identifiable seam. That's what makes them **set-in sleeves**, as opposed to inappropriate **raglan sleeves**.

Short-sleeve shirts have their place in society, but they do not belong in business or the professions. Call me a monarchist, but them's the facts. The worst that can happen is that I'll be shot in the revolution. **Short-sleeve shirts** are for grocers and exterminators. Wear one and people will look for your name in red, embroidered in script over the flap on your **pocket**.

fig. 15. Epaulets may make the man, but they most assuredly do not make a dress shirt. Consider adding a spiky little helmet. They *might* let you handle the canisters of mustard gas, but count on nothing when you're wearing epaulets.

If you live in the sun belt, you may take off your jacket. You may feel perfectly free to roll up your **sleeves**. ("Creative" people should do this all the time; it gives the general impression of boldness and iconoclasm.) But you may not opt for **short-sleeve dress shirts.**

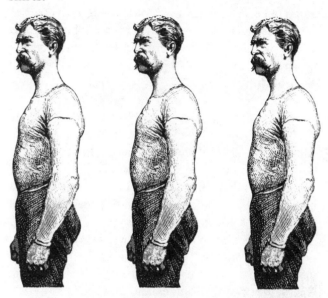

fig. 16. A short-sleeve shirt will make you look like any one of several hairy nineteenth-century day laborers in ill-fitting homespun pants.

The **sleeves** themselves will terminate variously. A very good shirt will boast an elaboration sometimes referred to as a **gauntlet cuff.** Apart from the **button** on the **cuff** itself, there will be another **button** 3 1/2 inches above it that should be pulled through the hole in the **button placket**. This **button** exists to close the **pointed tab end**, the slit which is gathered together by the **cuff**.

The whole arrangement smacks of redundancy and it would take a Vreeland to figure it out. But I have to admit I like a nice **gauntlet**. You can't throw it down or run it like a real **gauntlet**, but it adds a certain *je ne sais quoi* to the garment. The alternative is a featureless **cuff/ no gauntlet**. All other things being equal, go with the extra **button**.

Speaking of the French (not my first preference), you may choose to wear your **cuffs** as they do. You may also take a liking to the resurgence of right-wing politics and the impaling of dead people on the handles of umbrellas. I'm really not very good company when it comes to the French, but they did lend their name to a particular kind of **cuff**. It's the kind without **buttons** that fastens with a **cufflink**.

I have nothing positive to say on this subject, so let me be as hostile as I possibly can. **French cuffs** are pretentious and despicable features that communicate Old World arrogance and moral corruptibility.

The person who wears them should be deported immediately and forced to work as a trash stabber in the Bois de Boulogne. The incongruity of the image is perfectly delicious: snowy **cuffs**, a big gold bijou on each, and a five-foot-long stick with a spike on the end. Couldn't happen to a nicer guy. If a dead person turns up, you could skewer him with your stick.

Thank God for **collars**: They're culturally neutral (sort of). The first thing to consider is how the **collar** is built. Faced with the choice of disease and a **fused collar**, I would be hard-pressed to make a quick decision. A so-called **fused collar** is some awful amalgam of cloth and mastic smashed together to approximate the look of a tailored garment. What you want is a real **sewn collar**, **single-needle stitched** by a living person (or at least a living person at a person-sized machine). I am partial to shirts that are also **double-track stitched**. That means two lines of stitching instead of one.

I am also partial to **button-down collars.** I wish I could say that they make for great-looking shirts, but it's on-again, off-again when it comes to looks. The defining characteristic here is that the **points** of the **collar** fasten by **button** to the body of the shirt. Some ties work and some ties don't. The very worst combo is a little silk number that ties tight and neat against the throat. There's something weirdly sexual about the teeny little knot barely visible in the twin loops of the **collar**, but it doesn't do much for the faces of most men. Try to live your life as a person, as opposed to a flower painting by Georgia O'Keefe.

The right look for silk is the classic **Windsor spread collar** (also called a *col italien* in French). No **buttons** here, just stiff **points** of fabric. That usually means a shpritz or two of spray starch, but it depends entirely on your level of fastidiousness. You want a **collar** that will hold its shape without taking wing in the course of the day.

Spread collars and straight collars are slightly different versions of the same general attitude toward collars and points. Spread-collar shirts have a wider triangle of open space at the throat; straight-collar shirts a narrower triangle. Both kinds, however, really need to be starched; it's for precisely that reason that I never wear them and because both spread collars and straight collars need a suit or jacket. You can't make them work at your kid's preschool picnic; you'll look like The Father Who Is Never at Home.

fig. 17. A well-ironed collar may distract attention from other quirks and idiosyncracies. No one would notice that the man above has a slightly misshapen left earlobe.

That's what's nice about a **button-down shirt**. In a pinch you can wear it with jeans or shorts. **Straight-** and **spread-collar shirts** also fluctuate like hemlines. One year it's **points** that reach to Australia; the next year the **points** have been amputated to stubs. I won't even mention the current orthodoxy, because I'd like this book to stay current for at least thirteen years. By that time I'll be done with at least one set of tuition payments. The trick is to look at last November's *GQ*. Whatever month it is, look at last November. You'll get a rough idea of what real people are wearing without being duped by the high rollers in the Fashion Vanguard.

The third item in this series is **tab-collar shirts**. I like these very well because they work with every tie. There's a little fabric **tab** (get it?) halfway down the collar that functions like a tiny orthopedic device. When your tie goes limp it's there to catch it; you'll be tumescent all day long. Take a course in cultural anthropology if you'd like to know more about tumescence in ties.

The problem again is that part about formality: A **tab-collar shirt** needs a tie and jacket. If you try to wear one open, the dangle will do the talking. People will want to pull it off. Passing urologists will offer you a vasectomy. You may be the kind of person who wants that attention, but I write guides, not pornography.

CHAPTER EIGHT

HERE WE COME: A BACK LIKE A GOD

Heads up, class: We're ready to iron. You've got the tools, you speak the language, and there's a meeting tomorrow morning in Mergers and Acquisitions. RJR Nabisco wants to acquire the U.S. Senate and make a clean sweep of American government and industry.

You're their man and you'll do anything for a buck, but it could all go belly-up if the shirt don't cut it. Tobacco companies are sticklers for personal appearance. They don't particularly care about the color of your lungs, but you'd better show up in an ironed white shirt.

Where to begin? No doubt about it. It may never show beneath a suit or jacket, but the back of a shirt is the Beginning of Strength. Think of it as the Mother of Preparedness. If you initiate in weakness, you will end in sniveling. People will see you as a bag of offal, a loathsome holding tank of psychological imperfection.

Summon your resources and pull the shirt off the hanger. If you've done your job correctly, it will be lightly dimpled, with no major creases or deformations. Just enough of a challenge to raise your grain and bring out the best in male task-focus and responsiveness.

Now lay the shirt face down on the board. It should

hang inert, like an accident victim, with arms limp and dangling and no signs of life. If it rustles slightly, play with the horizontal adjustment. You may inadvertently have been transported into an alternative universe.

fig. 18. A finely ironed shirt makes the difference. Here it transforms a hobbit into a captain of industry. It's hardly noticeable that the braid on the chair is as long as his left femur.

The board itself will have two ends: the side that's square and the side that's tapered. For all practical purposes, there's only *one* side and it's exactly the opposite of what you might intuit. This is *man's* ironing, dammit, so stuff your intuition. If it's not accessible to reason, it is not accessible. The tapered end may be good for something in the world, but if it is, I haven't run into it. Maybe you could use it to iron coffee filters.

What *you* want is the blunt end of the board. The trick here is to pretend that the board is you, flattened and squared for the sake of convenience. The end of the board is the line of your shoulders; the sides of the board are the sides of your torso. Belly on up to the board in front of you, blunt end to the left, tapered to the right. Working now with grace and authority, snug the yoke of your shirt against the shoulders of the board. At the same time tug the back panel away from you.

If you've got any brain at all for following directions, two-thirds of the back will now be "boarded," with the remaining third dangling somewhere off the edge. All of this, of course, depends on your size. If you're the kind of man who is frequently mistaken for the Bullwinkle balloon in the Macy's parade, proportionately more of your shirt will dangle. The key is to begin *somewhere* with a plan in mind. The yoke of the shirt should be squared by the board, with the left seam of the back tugged hard against the edge.

Mirabile dictu we're ready to iron. Compose a short acrostic prayer based on the word "iron" ("**I**neffable One, **R**elease me from the **O**ppression of **N**itpickers") and give the boarded fabric a perfect little shpritz. Just enough to give the iron a little something to work with. Certify that the iron itself is plugged in and choose a setting to the high end of permanent press. You want the shirt to sizzle when you kiss it with steel. Cotton freaks will need to go higher; if you can't stand the heat, come home to a blend. Standing now with the tight edge in front of you, lay the hot metal down on the fabric.

You should immediately feel the power of the moment. The moisture in the shirt will vaporize on contact, creating a satisfying halo of real-guy steam. The iron itself will know what to do, smoothing, finishing, subduing the fabric. Wherever it goes it will trail magic behind: the clear, flat rightness of a well-ironed shirt.

Move the iron in whichever direction you please. Start with the yoke; start with tails; start in the middle near the pleat or the loop. It doesn't really matter what you iron first, and you may be tempted to return to the sectors you've completed. That's just as it should be on your maiden voyage. You should be drunk with the satisfaction of accomplishing something real. There's nothing evanescent about ironing a shirt. It's not a paper transaction or an electronic transfer. You can see your progress on the board in front of you. Enjoy the parts that give you pleasure. The rest of your life may be an endless humiliation, but here, truly, you can establish "flow."

Begin to concentrate on the center of the back. If there's a box pleat in the vicinity, nose carefully around it. Run the pointed end of the iron into the concave of each side, then flatten it hard with a manly swipe. As soon as you put the shirt on your back, the pleat will open like the folds of an accordion and ring out with the opening bars of the "Beer Barrel Polka." I swear to you, I've seen it happen.

fig. 19. As the iron touches the slightly moistened garment, the contact should produce a satisfying cloudlet of steam. This is a most impressive moment. Invite your friends to be present.

The iron itself should move like a figure skater: no scrapes, no slurs, no stutters or sluggishness. If the iron slows down, it may not be hot enough; there isn't enough oomph in an underperforming iron to vaporize the water and hydroplane to the finish.

If the iron seems to catch and bunch the fabric, the most probable cause is an iron that's *too* hot. If you're up in the stratosphere at the "cotton" or "linen" settings, the iron simply won't recognize the fabric beneath it. In a fastidious pique of elitist resentfulness, it will refuse to deal with your middle-class blend. The only remedy is to strike a blow for *égalité*. Cut the legs out from under your balky little debutante and lower the setting to the permanent press range.

By this time you're ready to do the rest of the panel. Draw the shirt back toward you and let the *other* seam catch on the end of the board furthest from where you're standing. Much of the fabric that you've already ironed will be laying docilely on the board in front of you. But you still need to deal with the un-ironed third.

At this point you should be sailboarding along, the wind at your back and the sun in your right hand. It will take just a pass or two to finish the job so that you can go on to more challenging sectors of the garment. Pause to admire the fruits of your labors: a crisply ironed back with no apologies to anyone.

CHAPTER NINE

THE FRONT BONE'S CONNECTED TO THE BACK BONE

I can feel it already: You're getting the hang of it. Long, smooth strokes in the wide open spaces; short, quick thrusts in the occasional tight corner. They make a wire attachment to keep the cord out of the way, but you're not the kind of guy who needs every little gimmick. Purity of line is the ticket here. What's an ironing board with a gallows arm to hold up the cord? A sturdy log cabin with a satellite dish mounted on the roof.

I feel the same way about the surface of the iron. They're using just about everything that duPont ever made. You've got your Teflon, your SilverStone, your who-knows-what. Next it will be some napalm derivative. I'm just your everyday purist with a taste for simple things. I don't want an iron that doubles as a crockpot. Give me a tool that does just one thing well: an iron with gravity and the glint of steel.

Very occasionally it will stick and burn, and you'll wind up with residue or a slight discoloration. Both can be removed with a pad of steel wool. Or else watch the catalogues for an iron-busting solvent. So what if it also busts the ozone layer? Which is more important: the environment or your tobacco company deal?

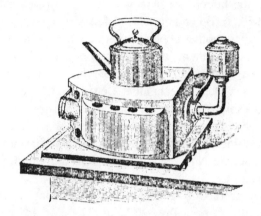

fig. 20. The dream of an iron that can do more than one thing predates Christianity. Here is a Meso-American iron/hot chocolate maker used in Aztec blood rituals.

Flip the shirt now and get ready for the front. Once again, the board is your body, rendered in two dimensions for the purpose of ironing. With the board in front of you, grab the front panel with the buttons, left hand on the top button and right hand on the tail, and "dress" the board as if it were you. The side seam will be snugged against the edge of the board, the bulk of the shirt will be dangling in front of you, and the front panel will be quietly awaiting your ministrations.

Now do what you were born to do: Shpritz the front

and let 'er rip. A couple of strokes should suffice for the open space, with lots of gentle temporizing in the area of the buttons. Imagine that the iron is a playful dolphin, nosing the buttons as if they were little rubber balls. Otherwise you'll end up with button remnants.

That's another good reason to do your own shirts. When you send them out, they may come back clean, but every other button will be broken or gone. The reason for this is a matter of technique: Before the dry-cleaner returns a shirt to you, he will have used it as a bib for his two-year-old son. From there to the pit bull and then to the coal mines. It's part of a federal program of fabric durability testing. No sweat for shirting, but the buttons just can't take it.

Be careful throughout to protect your gains. Ironing technology is basically sectional. The iron is small, you've only got one of them, but the shirt is just about as big as you are. You can only do one section at a time. That means that perfectly ironed panels will be dangled and draped after they're complete. With a little postmodern nurturance and gentleness, you should be able to handle the challenge. Exercise a little care and attention to detail and you'll end up with a shirt good enough to be buried in.

For the other front panel, slip the shirt off the board and drape it face-up across the opposite side. With your left hand at the top button and your right hand on the tail, snug down and toward you so that shirt is properly boarded. The bulk of the shirt will again be dangling, this time on the side of the board furthest from your body.

You need the seam along the board's edge and the corner in the sleeve tube. That way, you'll get the most bang for the buck.

The front panel now boarded should be a piece of cake. Shpritz and iron the single-ply fabric in the body and get the pocket to lay smooth and flat. If you iron toward the collar, there shouldn't be a problem; there's nothing at all to get in the way. Speaking *ex cathedra*, I probably shouldn't admit failure, but I almost always catch once on the downward stroke. This is no big deal: The pocket grabs the iron and the area simply has to be ironed again. (Shpritz a little extra to penetrate the two thicknesses.) I frankly feel that failure effectively humanizes me and should not properly interfere with your purchasing this book.

Spend a little extra time on the placket in the center. I know I said just the opposite above, but the placket calls to me like magnolias on a summer night. It has a seductive charm I cannot resist. It is like the Susan Sarandon character in *Bull Durham*.

Eventually it will be entirely obscured by your tie, but I see it as the centerpiece of the shirt as a whole. Shpritz it thoroughly and iron it with care. Think of this part as an act of centering, a focused involvement with the Zen of the shirt. Then think long and hard about Susan Sarandon. I can't help myself when it comes to the placket. It makes a mockery of rational thinking. It presses perversely toward inappropriate ideation. My best advice is to obsess away. The worst that can happen is that you will be institutionalized.

CHAPTER TEN

THE SLEEVE BONE'S CONNECTED TO THE FRONT BONE

As my channeler says when she tunes in to a tickle, "All right, there it is, we're getting *ready*." She does this with a throaty little growl to convince me that she's about to go out-of-body or something. If *you're* ready to lay the front panels aside, I'm ready to show you what to do with the sleeves.

I should mention in advance that there are a couple of possibilities. As it lays on the board, the sleeve is two layers thick. That's what happens when you flatten a tube. It means that everything on both sides will get ironed simultaneously.

The question is whether to flip and re-do. That depends on how many wrinkles got away from you the first time; how hot the iron is; and how thoroughly you shpritzed. The blessed are able to do sleeves in a single step, but you have to be a visible saint to succeed. Tibetan holy men have a fair shot at victory, but you really need to be a post-doctoral Peruvian shaman. No distractions and time to get organized. Just like anything else, sleeves take focus.

In either case, you begin the same way. Hold the collar in your left hand with your right hand on the right cuff and smooth the full length of the sleeve onto the board in front of you. Most everything will be dangling off the blunt end of the board with the sleeve and the right shoulder waiting to be ironed.

Take special pains to smooth the fabric. If you aren't making the kind of progress you expect, run your right arm up the tube of the sleeve. Spread your thumb and pinkie so that you are cursing in Italian and then bring your hand slowly out of the sleeve again. The trick is to drag your pinkie along the underarm seam. If your fingers are long enough, you will flatten the tube and clear the decks for successful ironing.

Now douse the fabric with Old Shpritz again and put some English into a few swipes of the iron. You'll need to press a little bit harder than usual to get the dimpling out of both layers of fabric.

I take idiosyncratic satisfaction out of doing this part because I like the way the sleeve fits the iron. It's just about as wide as the iron is long, so that you can zap the whole sleeve with each pass of the tool. The curve of the iron also rhymes with the shoulder seam. If you've got a thing for articulated parts, you may like that section as well as I do. If you think that's strange, you should have seen me as a child. It's amazing I made it to my thirteenth birthday.

What applies to sleeves applies also to cuffs: an extra shpritz and special pressure on the iron. Remember that you're working now with four layers of fabric. The cuff itself is two-ply for structure and flattening the tube makes four layers altogether. With a little conviction you should be able to bring it off. This part is *directly* related to the size of your endowment. Insecure men should open the cuff section flat and never even try to do more than two-ply at once.

fig. 21. The wrong approach to the poorly ironed sleeve. It is inappropriate to have your arm amputated as penance for failure.

When you're done with the first pass examine the sleeve closely. If you're satisfied with the results, you're ready to go on. If not, lay the sleeve facedown on the board and do the back of the sleeve just like the front. Don't be discouraged if you need to flip. Tom Selleck *never* gets it right the first time. Neither do other icons of masculinity. That's a comfort to me as I'm sure it will be to you. As personal ironing trainer to the stars, I know whereof I speak.

Once you're truly satisfied, go on to the left sleeve. It's just more of the same, so I'll keep it short. Depending on how you board the sleeve, you'll be ironing the back or the front of the tube. I've got another thing for fearful symmetry, so I like to begin with the front of the sleeve. It wouldn't hurt you to be more like me, so I'll advocate strongly for this approach. Reader and author should be strongly identified. Don't you think it's better that way?

CHAPTER ELEVEN

A Short Disquisition on Human Suffering

Thanks so very much for buying this book. Commercial success has been profoundly gratifying and I relish the opportunity to pay so many of my bills. Beans and rice were grand at the beginning, but how much fatigue can a palate take?

It seems right to mention that a book like this one can only convey a fraction of my gifts. A man like me wears many hats: Ideal Father, Sexual God, Natural Athlete, Image of the Divine. Have I mentioned my career at the University of Michigan? Phi Beta Kappa in my junior year. Charles Angell scholar six semesters running.

Why, then, do the righteous suffer? We live in a world created for human habitation by an Entity respectful of our freedom and prerogatives. That same Entity dwells apart, in a parallel realm of perfection and holiness. The task of human life is to accept this imbalance and realize that it is fraught with possibilities for self-realization. The price of divine withdrawal is that many of us will suffer. The wonder of this arrangement is that we can be responsible actors in the drama of a relationship with a Force beyond our own.

I'm glad we had this little moment together. Being a publishing animal has been hard on my self-image. I have begun to feel intellectually wasted. If you'd like to hear more, please write my publisher. They're thinking about signing me for books on sewing and housecleaning. Mama didn't raise me to be an intellectual whore.

CHAPTER TWELVE

THE COLLAR BONE'S CONNECTED TO THE HUMAN SUFFERING BONE

Glory be, it's the home stretch already. Stick with me, Junior, and you'll be irresistible. The Senate will hand *itself* to RJR Nabisco for the pure pleasure of watching you in action.

Gently grab your shirt by the shoulders, carefully protecting your hard-won gains. By that I mean no rough stuff or carelessness. If you've done your job, you're holding a well-ironed shirt. Banging it around will get you nothing except a topographical map of the Missouri Breaks.

With most of the shirt dangling at your waist, lay the yoke down in front of you in the center of the board. You want the shirt faceup, flat on its back. Now adjust the collar so that it's also flat. This is almost impossible, given the construction of the shirt, but try to do the best you can. The collar band itself will buckle slightly, but that won't interfere with the work you're about to do.

By this time, there won't be much washer moisture left, so you'll have to be serious about moistening the collar. Shpritz it to hell and don't look back. Be careful to check also for removable stays. Those are the little strips of celluloid that keep a spread collar stiff. It's best to remove them before the shirt is washed, but when you reach this point it's do or die.

fig. 22. Collar stays come in a variety of shapes and sizes. Some people insist that they are good for snacking. I personally think that you should never use a stay larger than your head.

If you iron the collar with the shirt stays in, the fabric surrounding the stay will turn slick and shiny. Tobacco people hate that look; it reminds them of the moral quality of their lives.

I would like to say a word about shirts with permanent stays, but the words will not cross the barrier of my lips. Permanent stays are unworthy of consideration; my advice on the subject is simply unprintable.

Now lift the iron and steam press the collar. Move back and forth until it looks just right. A badly made shirt will drop a cow pie right here. The typical problem is mismatched panels: The two layers of the collar will be poorly cut or sewn, and it will be impossible to keep the fabric flat. One layer will pucker and refuse to sit quietly. You'll probably end up beating it back, but it will resemble nothing so much as well-ironed blister. Serves you right for false economies.

Spend a few bucks on a decent dress shirt and you'll get a collar that makes you look like a CEO. Think of the advantages when they serve the summons. Nobody likes a slovenly inside trader. If you're going to be a criminal, be a *real* white-collar criminal. The mini-cam report will make you look like a dream.

CHAPTER THIRTEEN

THE GAINS

I once heard a reverie about ironing-as-pleasure. All I could think of was a dioxin cocktail or a concrete abutment, whichever would end my misery quicker.

There *is* something nice about the smell of ironing and the satisfaction that comes of doing it yourself. Some guys get off on the iconography of bachelorhood. It's the tape where you stand in your boxers on a cold December morning, watching the *Today Show* with a cup of coffee close by, ironing the shirt you're about to put on.

It's like those surrealist ads for Paco Rabanne they keep running in *The New York Times Magazine*. A half-naked guy on a porch in the woods, writing screenplays while he chats with his baby in The City, tossing off thirty double entendres in a row. They don't do that well on the Centre Court at Wimbledon.

The bachelors I know aren't bachelors anymore. They live in houses that need to be reshingled, with children who could open cans with a whisper. There's no money for anything and no time for what's left: just the sound of guinea pigs whimpering in distress as their little aquarium fills with scat. I'd like to see the Paco Rabanne guy cutting fallen tree branches into precise four-foot lengths so that the sanitation engineers will condescend to pick them up.

Ironing itself is basically O.K. It's better than spending a year in a deep shaft coal mine and beats handling radioactive waste without protective clothing. But it should *not* be construed as an Aesthetic Experience or a milestone on the road to self-actualization. I find delusional thinking almost always nauseating, even if it might help to sell this book.

Neither will it make you more attractive to women. There was an odd little interlude during the early 1970s when people began to blather about new ways of think-ing. A small group of women on 58th Street in Manhat-tan announced to their men friends that it was O.K. to be nurturant. They said that men could have the courage to be domestic; that they would *love them better* if they were less gender-specific.

Suddenly everyone was talking this way. Camera crews came to 58th Street and beamed the new message to Omaha and Seattle. It was no longer a matter of tribal rites in Manhattan, but a national craze for the abandon-ment of machismo. CEOs quit their jobs in droves, begging for work as assistant cookie monitors in what-ever day-care centers would employ them. Rocket scien-tists plugged liquid hydrogen leaks by day and bottled tarragon vinegar at night. On weekends they blew deco-rative glass decanters to hold the surplus of their Tues-day-night production runs.

Everywhere men strove to be sensitive and gentle, to box and bury their penile selves. I know men who began to talk of "quality time," who took new inspira-tion from *la vie domestique*. Men without children abandoned their briefcases and took their papers to work in denim Snuglis, just to be part of the contemporary *Zeitgeist*. Some took up housekeeping in quasi-earnest, making puff pastry by the metric ton and sewing curtains for the mistress bedroom. *Some even did a load of laundry* and made a few tentative swipes with an iron.

fig. 23. An early 1970s dream of sexual achievement through ironing. "She will overlook my faults and pledge herself to me utterly if I reveal my considerate feminine side."

I rush to inform you that it was all a lie. Those hapless shmucks on 58th Street didn't get better lovin' from anyone. They got marginalized in forty-eight hours, pushed aside by their aspiring women. "What's more fun," the women asked, "a business lunch at Windows on the World, or choosing the right disposable diaper?" It's amazing that it didn't happen sooner and amazing that the men were so utterly dumb.

American women didn't want nurturance; they just didn't want to have to be nurturant themselves. Since *somebody* has to wipe Baby's butt, they tricked us men into doing it for them, all the while talking incantatorily about "tapping the wellspring of the feminine in all of us."

All of this may sound like penile pique, but I don't really hold anyone responsible. I behaved for years like I thought I was supposed to, long after the Manhattan men got it together. I was just too far away, in Kansas City, to hear them making their pitiful little squeaks as their squalid aquariums filled up with scat. I tried nurturance, I tried domesticity, hoping that my woman would love me better, if only I could put aside the things that made me: arrogance, task-focus, gross insensitivity. I even thought that ironing would help. It would clinch the deal on the new social order.

My woman wanted none of this, or if she did, she wanted other things more: financial security, discretionary spending, and a husband who could combine masterful reliability with a willingness kindly to stay out of her face. The sensitive domestic stuff was simply a ruse to loosen my hold on legitimate authority.

In the meantime, we are still Voyagers in Life,

but it's been so long getting here, I can't be certain.

The trick is to watch what the iron is doing. Lay each leg separately on the surface of the board, just as if it were an exceptionally long sleeve. Take excruciating pains to straighten the crease; unless you'd like to look like Mississippi in the 30s, carelessness here could cost you big time.

fig. 24. As the tobacco company deal comes to a close, beware of loose ends and unresolved details. The bodyguard of the CEO is likely to beat you to death with his stick for any incongruities in the language of the agreement.

My best advice is to lay the *outside* of the leg face-down on the board and begin to iron on the *inside* panel. That way, a disaster will be somewhat less noticeable. Moisten very gently and start right in. Just as with sleeves, you are ironing a tube: Both panels of fabric have to be smoothed when you board them.

Let me pause to recommend an old-timey technique to avoid that business of snail spoor on the fabric. In olden times, before the Pleistocene period, people used something called an "ironing cloth." According to the sages, this was a length of fabric woven from the hair of philo-Semitic Germans. There were probably only two or three in existence and each was subjected to regular abuse. They were placed between the garment and the iron so that the iron never touched the garment itself. This kept the iron from mashing the fabric even as it accomplished its lofty purpose.

Real ironing cloths are now a thing of the past. The French couldn't stand the idea of philo-Semitic Germans and collaborated in having them deported to the East. But you can accomplish the same with a piece of pillowcase or any thin fabric that won't absorb a lot of heat. The trick is to create a permeable barrier that will let the heat through but keep the metal off the garment. Let me know if you find something that works particularly well. I'd be glad to credit you in the next edition.

For casual trousers, skip the ironing cloth. A little spot of shine won't matter much at all. Twills, poplins, and cotton wash pants should be boarded like dress trousers, laying on their sides so as to create a center crease. Don't be saddened by the image of your prostrate trousers, depleted and gasping while they wait for your attention. They'll perk up plenty when they feel the heat.

fig. 25. Dutiful Rhine *mädchen* spinning strands of hair from her philo-Semitic lover.

Corduroys and denims can be done the same way, though it may be a tiny bit pretentious to go for the center crease. There's a measure of integrity in boarding them differently, like a child's front-on picture of a pair of pants. The side- and in-seams will be on either side of the leg, and you'll iron over the kneecaps and the front of the thighs. I leave the choice entirely to you. Some people love to be pretentious SOBs.

fig. 26. The disastrous effects of inattention to detail while ironing dress pants. A good strong source of fluorescent lighting would have helped. Problems like this may run in a family. The man on the right apparently learned nothing from his older brother's mistakes.

For the part near your privates, you're on your own. There's no good way to run a normal iron through the minefield of complexities between the groin and the waistband. You can stick the pointed end of the board into your pants and try ironing half of your butt at a time. Then flip things over and try to do the front. I wish you well, but I have no patience for this. Things deteriorate for me in Pleat Land and Fly Canyon. I simply can't work it out to my own satisfaction, let alone impress a tobacco company exec.

I figure I'm saving so much money on the shirts I iron, I can afford to send the goddam pants to the cleaners. Take your pick between frugality and neatness. Me, I'd go with neatness every time.

CHAPTER FIFTEEN

A WEIRD HINT

A cousin of mine has a clangorously idiosyncratic wife who freezes his shirts before she irons them. She also dresses entirely in red and wears a Zuñi fetish through one pierced nostril. I meant what I said about idiosyncratic.

Her theory on freezing is that each filament of the fabric is rectified in the great violence of the contact between iron and ice. There's poetry here; of that I am certain. And it is strangely impressive to see her wad a wet shirt and pop it between the Häagen-Dazs and the orange juice concentrate. There is a sense of crossing the border of normalcy into a world where things might be seductively different. Then again I also dress entirely in red and wear a Zuñi fetish through one pierced nostril.

I have to admit that her technique seems to work. I'd envy *anyone* with a wife who did the ironing, but his shirts make mine look like a nickel on the dollar. Every one of them is a snow leopard of whiteness, crisply ironed and arranged just so. The collars alone are miracles of rightness, as if each bore the touch of an angelic hand.

Let us note in passing the surpassing irony of this marriage between weirdness and utter conventionality.

Nothing could be more strange than freezing your wash and nothing more ordinary than an ironed white shirt. This is what we mean by the Zen of the Everyday. Such is the path to simple perfection.

CHAPTER SIXTEEN

WHERE TO FROM HERE?

By now you're probably saying, "This Williams guy is great. Where can I get more books like this one?"

I'd like you to buy my other books, but I regret to say that they haven't been written. I've got a whole series planned on the basic tasks of life: *Sewing A Button, Organizing Your Closet, Raising Your Children, Abandoning Your Aged Parents*. All will no doubt be absolutely delightful, but I can't afford to write them without a hefty advance.

My best advice is to write to my publishers and demand that they give me the encouragement I deserve. There's no time like the present to do me a good turn; don't let this enchanted moment pass.

If you happen to be a publisher yourself, I would be glad to write my books for you. Just send me a letter in care of the people who published this book and make me an offer we both can live with. I feel grateful, of course, to the nice people here, but loyalty has never been my particular strength. Nothing would suit me like a nice little bidding war. I think it would be fun for all of us, don't you?

ENDPAPER

fig. 27. Cross-dressing career man ironing like the dickens. Note five o'clock shadow on left side of face.